# Ed Roberts: Wheelchair Genius
**1st print edition, revised**

## by Steven E. Brown

©2006, Revised 2015, by the Institute on Disability Culture.
All rights reserved. Printed in the United States of America.

No portion of this publication may be reproduced, copied or transmitted in any form or by any means, electronic or mechanical, including photocopying, recording, or by any information storage and retrieval system, without permission in writing from the publisher except in the case of brief quotations embodied in critical reviews and certain other noncommercial uses permitted by copyright law.

ISBN: 13: 978-1-931145-06-0

$9.99

For further information, see the Institute on Disability Culture website at:
www.instituteondisabilityculture.org

Cover Photo: Ed, in his office, at the World Institute on Disability, in Oakland, California, looking at a picture of himself and his son, Lee.

While many people helped develop this book
the two most important contributors were Ed and Zona Roberts.

This work is dedicated to Ed's memory and to Zona.

# TABLE OF CONTENTS

| | |
|---|---|
| THE EMPTY BLUE WHEELCHAIR | 1 |
| "I DON'T KNOW HOW WE'RE GOING TO DO IT, BUT WE'RE GONNA DO IT!" | 3 |
| JELLO SALADS | 5 |
| POLIO | 7 |
| RESTING ON A CLOUD | 11 |
| STARING AT A STAR | 14 |
| TOO CRIPPLED TO WORK | 17 |
| THE ROLLING QUADS | 21 |
| THE PHYSICALLY DISABLED STUDENTS PROGRAM | 24 |
| THE DISABILITY RIGHTS MOVEMENT | 27 |
| GENIUS | 32 |
| LEGACIES | 36 |
| PHOTO CREDITS | 41 |
| ACKNOWLEDGEMENTS | 42 |
| ABOUT THE AUTHOR | 43 |

# LIST OF PHOTOGRAPHS

| | |
|---|---|
| Ed's last wheelchair, now at the Smithsonian Institution, in Washington, D.C | **2** |
| Ed as a toddler | **4** |
| Ed, as a teenager, and his iron lung | **8** |
| Herb Willsmore and Ed Roberts | **23** |
| Governor Jerry Brown and Ed | **29** |
| Ed Roberts, Joan Leon, Judy Heumann | **32** |
| Ed, near the end of his life | **38** |

# CHAPTER 1
## THE EMPTY BLUE WHEELCHAIR

The empty blue wheelchair seemed to float in the air.

This chair was no stranger to us. Our friend, Ed Roberts, used this wheelchair during the last years of his life.

My wife, Lillian, and I were in Washington, D.C., in the summer of 1995, for a conference. We rolled, in our wheelchairs, out of the large hotel elevator. When we turned the corner, our breath caught in our throats.

The empty blue wheelchair sat in front of us.

Just weeks before, Lillian and I had traveled to California. We joined a thousand other people in a huge gymnasium at the University of California at Berkeley. People from all over the world came to celebrate Ed's life.

I first met Ed in the fall of 1990. Lillian met him in the late 1970s. When Ed died unexpectedly, maybe from a heart attack, but no one knows for sure, on March 14, 1995, we both lost a friend, co-worker, and teacher.

Thousands of other people all over the world felt the same way.

Why did so many people love Ed? This is his story—the tale of a twentieth-century hero.

*Ed's Wheelchair at the Hyatt Regency Hotel Bethesda, Maryland*

# CHAPTER 2
## "I DON'T KNOW HOW WE'RE GOING TO DO IT, BUT WE'RE GONNA DO IT!"

Ed's story begins with a little bit of history about his family. Ed's mom, Zona, didn't have a happy childhood. Her mother married several times and moved many times while Zona was still a child. Zona imagined a different kind of life for herself and her own family.

Zona met Verne Roberts during her senior year in high school. They both lived near San Francisco, California. They fell in love and married in 1938, shortly after Zona graduated from high school.

Verne's father, Walter, fixed machines for the Southern Pacific Railroad. Verne worked for the railroad too. He did whatever chores someone found for him. Jobs and money didn't come easily to most people during those times known as the "Great Depression." One out of every four people who wanted to work could not find a job.

Edward Verne Roberts weighed about six pounds when he was born on January 23, 1939. After Zona and Ed stayed in the hospital for about a week, they returned to their home in Burlingame, south of

San Francisco. As new parents, they were both excited and nervous about the changes a baby would bring to their lives. Zona said, "Well, here we are--I don't know how we're going to do it, but we're gonna do it!"

*An early family photo of Ed*

## CHAPTER 3
### JELLO SALADS

Zona wanted her children to be happy. She needed skills, like cooking, for this to happen. When Zona first married, all she could make were jello salads and cakes. Verne often walked to his nearby mother's house, where he could always enjoy a pot of soup.

Ed walked and talked early. He said his first word, "kitty-cat," when he was about nine months old.

He ran everywhere, just like his father did. Verne liked running so much he once chased a dog around the block to get him back into the house. Ed didn't sit still long enough to learn to read until the fifth grade.

A day after her twenty-second birthday, Zona gave birth to the family's second son, Ron. He looked like a Gerber baby-blonde and gorgeous. Ron, three years younger than Ed, grew up following his brother across the street to play.

Verne spent much of his time at home in the garage fixing things or gardening. Everyone in the neighborhood knew him as someone who lent a helping hand.

Zona joined community groups, like the Parent Teacher Association (PTA). She even became PTA President.

Mark, the third son in the family, was born when Ed was about twelve and Ron about nine. The couple's fourth and final child, another son, Randy, arrived two and half years later.

Sports, like baseball and football, seemed perfect for a child like Ed, who usually wanted to be in motion. Ed liked school because he could play there. At recess he was the center of activity and attention. After school he played at the high school playground across from the Roberts's house.

Ed had lots of energy and used most of it playing football whenever he could. At other times, he helped his father around the house. For example, one year Ed worked with Verne and Ron to repair their roof.

Zona had a hard time getting Ed to go to bed because he still had so much energy. Life with four boys in the family was a busy one. Ed got his share of scrapes and bruises but that was expected in their active world.

Their life was a typical one in the early 1950s. Little did they know how quickly that would all change.

# CHAPTER 4
## POLIO

Many people don't know about polio today because few people in the U.S. have had it. But in the first half of the 1900s polio was a serious disease. Medical researchers developed vaccines to prevent polio in the 1950s and 1960s. By the 1960s, people all over the U.S. were able to take a pill to vaccinate them from polio.

Polio is a virus, like the flu. Not everyone had the same physical reaction. Some people who got polio did not get very sick at all. Other people became really sick, in different ways, just like with the flu. In the 1940s and 1950s, thousands of Americans got sick from polio. Many people died from this disease. Others survived, but with various kinds of disabilities.

In 1953, when Ed was 14, he was a star athlete at his school. He dreamed of playing professional sports. One afternoon, after playing baseball, Ed came home saying he wasn't feeling well.

The next morning Ed woke up with a fever and a sore spine, or backbone. A doctor came at dinnertime to examine Ed. He wanted to take Ed to a nearby hospital right away. The doctor thought Ed might have polio.

Ed walked into the hospital. He got up once during his first night to go to the bathroom. He never walked again.

Two days later he couldn't breathe. They rushed him into an iron lung, a machine as big as a small car, which could breathe for him.

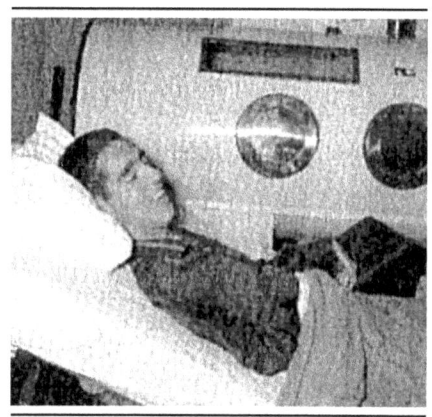

*Ed, in front of his iron lung.*

The iron lung, which looked like a tunnel on wheels, moved a person's chest and lungs. It supplied the force necessary to breathe. When the iron lung pushed in on someone's body their lungs released air. When it stopped pushing, the body relaxed and breathed in. Ed spent at least twelve hours, half of each day, in the iron lung, his entire body, except his head, inside the machine.

Ed devoted a lot of time while he was in the hospital learning how to breathe when he was not in the iron lung. This was called "frog-breathing." He swallowed air like a frog--using his tongue and throat to push air into his lungs. This took a lot of energy.

The polio virus caused permanent damage to Ed's body. Sometimes polio harmed the central nervous system and the spinal cord, destroying muscles and movement. Some people lost their ability to move their leg muscles. They needed to use crutches or a wheelchair. Other people lost the use of muscles in their arms. They needed assistance using silverware or turning the pages of a book.

Ed became paralyzed in most of his body. He had little control of any of his muscles. He became a quadriplegic, or quad, someone whose arms and legs are paralyzed. He could move only two fingers on his left hand and two toes on his left foot. The rest of his body, including his lungs, remained paralyzed. He could only breathe by himself using frog-breathing, which he couldn't do for long.

Ed spent several years in hospitals after getting sick with polio. During Ed's first year in the hospital, Verne and Zona decided to take a vacation. They left for a week to visit friends in northern California. This was quite far from the hospital where Ed stayed.

Leaving Ed like this was difficult. But when Zona discussed this trip years later, she recalled that because Ed lived through that week, she believed he could deal with whatever the future brought.

Ed also thought that trip helped him get better. Polio had caused enough pain in his life. If his parents gave up their own lives because of him, he could not bear it. He was glad they chose to take that vacation.

After Ed got over being sick from the virus he had to learn how to do lots of simple things, like dressing and eating, all over again, or letting other people know how and when to help him. The family learned about a program that taught these skills at Children's Hospital in San Francisco. Ed's parents moved him there in the back of their station wagon.

In the new hospital, Ed stopped eating. Zona watched a nurse nag Ed about food and talked to a psychologist, who in turn suggested the nurse leave Ed alone.

Ed's attitude changed when the pressure was off. He started to eat. Later in life, he often talked about how powerful the mind can be in both sickness and health. When he decided he wanted to eat, he did. But no one else could force him to want to eat. He needed to make that decision on his own.

# CHAPTER 5
## RESTING ON A CLOUD

Ed was ready to go back home after spending several years in hospitals, and learning how live in this body that now did everything in a new way. The upcoming change frightened Zona. She saw all the things that people helped Ed with in the hospital. She worried she would be so busy with Ed she would never again be able to leave the house.

She shared these feelings with a nurse. The nurse was surprised no one told Zona about the Polio Foundation. The Foundation organized and paid for help for families with someone who had polio. Assistance could be as much as four hours per day five days a week.

After Zona learned about the Polio Foundation she felt calmer about the many changes to come.

The family moved into a new home because their old house didn't have room for Ed's iron lung and other equipment. In the new house the large dining room became Ed's bedroom.

With Ed home from the hospital, the family began a new routine. Verne got up early to go to work.

Mrs. Hibner, from the Polio Foundation, came to help out in the house. Verne returned home from work in the afternoon. Zona had dinner ready about 5:00 o'clock.

Before dinner, Ed got a bath. It took two people to transfer Ed from his bed to a bath. One person used one arm to hold his head and the other arm to support Ed's arms and upper back. A second person supported Ed's lower back and under his knees.

Verne's ability to work with machines made life easier for the family. He could wake up in the middle of the night, fix any kind of problem with the iron lung, and go back to sleep.

Ed felt most relaxed when he lay in his iron lung. The lung became his lifelong friend. He would get into it at night. During the day he used a portable breathing machine, called a respirator, attached to his manual wheelchair.

Ed had to spend at least twelve hours in the iron lung to feel good the next day. He once said that being in the iron lung felt like resting on a cloud, soft and warm. Since he didn't have to focus on breathing, he could give attention to other matters.

No one else in Ed's school had polio. High school classes began again for Ed when he was 18, four years after getting polio. He used a phone hook-up provided by the local phone company and the Women's Club. When Ed pushed a bar on the phone, with his left foot, he could be heard and when he let go of the bar, he could hear. That way he could not only listen but also talk to his classmates.

One monthly phone bill that went to every customer contained an insert about Ed. It included his picture and a short article about how he used the phone hook-up to go to school. This began a lifetime of publicity about Ed.

## CHAPTER 6
### STARING AT A STAR

At home, when Ed wanted to read a book or magazine it was placed on a raised bed tray. He used a mouthstick, a long stick he held between his teeth, to turn the pages himself. Ed listened to the constant activity of his busy home. He watched TV. Many visitors came into Ed's open area in the middle of the house. Since he couldn't leave, he learned how to tune out what he didn't want to hear and fall asleep. This became a lifelong habit.

Once a semester, Ed's high school class met at his house. During Ed's senior year, Zona told him he had to attend classes once a week at the high school. Ed was scared. He hadn't been to the school since the 8th grade.

His greatest fear was people staring at him. He eventually decided if people were always going to stare at him, he would work to be a star.

Ed graduated from high school, at the age of twenty, in 1959. But not without a fight. He had gone back to school as quickly as he could, but since he couldn't move his arms or legs Ed didn't take Physical Education (P.E.) classes or learn to drive.

The school required these two courses for students to graduate. They were not going to let Ed graduate from high school because he had not taken these courses.

Zona wanted her son to be as much like everyone else as possible. She had a difficult time accepting his high school treating Ed this way. She called the principal to protest this decision, but without success. Then she contacted a friend who was on the school board.

Someone from the school met with Zona and Ed at their home. He asked, "Ed, you wouldn't like a cheap diploma, would you?"

The school officials thought Ed should attend all the classes the other students did. This included P.E. and driver's education. They said if he did not, then his diploma would not be as meaningful.

An angry Zona got in touch with the Superintendent of Schools, whom she knew from PTA work. She also called some of Ed's teachers.

They planned to support his graduation at a school board meeting. But before they did anything, the

School Board decided to award Ed his diploma based on the quality of his work.

After the graduation ceremony there was a big party at the Roberts's home. Everyone celebrated Ed's success.

Zona thought Ed gained a lot out of watching her fight for his graduation. Ed learned how important it was to fight for what he believed in.

# CHAPTER 7
## TOO CRIPPLED TO WORK

After high school, Ed started going to classes at a local community college. He got into a big back brace so he could sit up while going to classes. The brace, which sat above his waist, included a part to hold his head up high. A machine, called a respirator, was attached to the back of his manual wheelchair. It helped him breathe outside of the iron lung.

Zona drove Ed to campus. They would then ask strangers for help to get Ed in and out of the car. Once at college, Ed went to classes by himself, asking other students to help him. After awhile, Zona and Ed hired another student to drive Ed back and forth to campus.

Ed took a lot of time to get around campus and to do homework. He needed three years to finish two years of class work. While he studied, Ed thought about what he wanted to do with his life.

He considered becoming a sportswriter. But he decided he wanted to learn how government worked. He chose political science, the study of politics.

Both Ed and Zona met one of the most important

people in their lives when Ed took an English class during his second semester. A lady named Jean Wirth taught the class. Jean, like Ed, knew how it felt when people stared. She had been six feet, five inches tall from the time she was twelve years old.

One day, Jean asked Ed which University he wanted to attend after graduating from community college.

He replied the University of California at Los Angeles (UCLA). He thought it would be a friendly place for him and his wheelchair. A lot of war veterans who had been hurt went there.

Jean didn't like that idea. UCLA was a commuter campus, meaning people lived off campus, at home or in apartments. Ed would have to find a place to live, get rides to school, and find friends away from the university.

She suggested he apply to the University of California at Berkeley (Cal). He could live on campus and the school had an excellent political science program.

Ed took Jean's advice and applied to Cal. The form he filled out asked no questions about disability. Cal accepted Ed.

Ed also asked the California Department of Rehabilitation (DOR) for financial aid. DOR helped people with disabilities get training or education so they could work one day.

Ed's DOR caseworker told him his disability was so severe he would never be able to work. He refused to help Ed. Several people, including Zona and Jean, fought with DOR about this decision. They won. DOR gave Ed some money to help with school costs.

Jean, Zona, and Ed visited the Cal campus before the school year began. People at the university were shocked when they met Ed.

These administrators thought there were two big problems. None of the campus dormitory rooms, where students lived, could support his heavy iron lung. They were also scared about what might happen to Ed if his equipment failed.

The first problem was more difficult. Ed was going to hire people, called personal assistants or PAs, to help him with his equipment and to push his wheelchair across campus. But where could he live?

Someone at the University suggested they talk to Henry Bruyn. He was a doctor at Cowell Hospital, the campus student health center. Dr. Bruyn worked with lots of people who had polio. He thought they should be able to go to college. He believed Ed could live at Cowell. For the rest of the summer, everyone thought about ways Ed could successfully live at the student hospital while taking college courses.

# CHAPTER 8
## THE ROLLING QUADS

Ed stayed in Berkeley for most of the 1960s. In the beginning he was the only student living at Cowell Hospital. People believe he was the first student with his type of disability to go to an American university.

Ed started school in Berkeley in the fall of 1962. A local paper had a story about Ed with the headline, "Helpless Cripple Goes to School."

In a nearby town, a social worker read the story. Social workers help people to live better lives. This social worker assisted a student named John Hessler (there's more about John in the next chapter). John had broken his neck in a diving accident. Like Ed, John was a quad who used a wheelchair, and like Ed had, John attended a community college.

John's social worker got him in touch with Cal and helped him apply for school and move into Cowell. He joined Ed at Cowell in the beginning of the 1963 school year.

The Cowell program added more students with disabilities in the next few years. At Cowell Hospital, each student had his or her own room. They could all gather in a big room to talk or watch TV. They spent a lot of time together discussing their lives and providing support for each other. After a few years they even gave themselves a name, the Rolling Quads.

While Ed was in Berkeley, his father, Verne, who had been strong and healthy, became tired in the summer of 1963. The doctors said Verne, who had smoked most of his life, had lung cancer. It had already spread over most of his body.

Verne went into the hospital early in 1964. Doctors told Zona that Verne would soon die. They were right. The cancer spread to Verne's brain.

He passed away in February 1964. He was forty-seven years old. Verne and Zona had been married for twenty-seven years.

After Verne died, Zona began going to community college. When she finished, she too wanted to go to Berkeley.

Zona moved there in 1967, when she was forty-seven. She loved Berkeley. Her new house became known as the "green house" for its outside paint job. There were always people there, including Ed, who visited once in a while.

When Zona earned her degree in 1969, her sons gave her a graduation present of a trip to Europe for three months. After she got back, she went to school for one more year. She earned her teaching certificate in 1970.

*Herb Willsmore and Ed Roberts, Rolling Quads, about 1969*

# CHAPTER 9
## THE PHYSICALLY DISABLED STUDENTS PROGRAM

Zona lived happily in Berkeley in the late 1960s. But Ed tired of this city. He had finished all his undergraduate and graduate classes. He longed to do something else. Ed learned the University of California at Riverside, near Los Angeles, wanted someone to run their student services program. Ed got the job.

Ed got ready to go to Riverside. Before he left, Jean Wirth called Zona to say the government had a lot of money for college students. Ten percent of the money was just for disability programs. Jean suggested Zona travel to meetings in Washington to learn how to use the money. Zona couldn't go, so she suggested Jean call Ed. Jean did and Ed agreed to go.

Ed's trip to Washington was a big deal. He had never traveled on an airplane with his breathing equipment. He didn't know what it would be like to do so. As it turned out, he had to breathe on his own on this long trip. He was really tired after using his frog-breathing. Once he got to Washington, the hotel where he and his brother Mark, who had traveled with him, were scheduled to stay wouldn't let Ed bring his iron lung. They were afraid it would blow up!

Jean Wirth located a hotel that would accept Ed's iron lung and the two brothers stayed there. Despite the hardships of this trip, Ed learned he could travel long distances and he did for the rest of his life. He traveled all over the world.

Ed also loved Washington. He met lots of important people, like Senators and Representatives. Ed felt he made a big impression on these people. He thought they would remember him for a long time.

When Ed got back to California after these meetings, he shared what he had learned. Ed talked John Hessler and others into asking the government for some of the money being offered for college students. They would start a program helping others learn how to go to school successfully, just like the Rolling Quads.

They started a program for Cal students called the Physically Disabled Students Program (PDSP). It was the first of its kind in the world.

John Hessler became Director of the program. PDSP helped students with transportation and personal assistance at school and in the home. The first group of PAs (personal assistants) came from all over the United States. Some PAs were people called "conscientious objectors." They chose to become PAs instead of becoming soldiers and fighting in Vietnam. This is a country in Southeast Asia, where the U.S. fought in a war that many people did not support.

PDSP also helped students with repairs of their wheelchairs, such as changing flat tires, fixing motors, or changing batteries. This was important because students who used wheelchairs couldn't go to class if they couldn't get around.

Zona worked half time at PDSP while she looked for a teaching job. At PDSP, Zona drove people to and from campus and helped people who needed emergency personal assistance. She was on call night and day. She managed these services when she returned to school to get a Master's degree.

Ed, meanwhile, did not stay in Riverside long. He had trouble breathing there so he moved back to the Bay Area.

## CHAPTER 10
**THE DISABILITY RIGHTS MOVEMENT**

People with disabilities from all over the San Francisco area wanted help from the Physically Disabled Students Program (PDSP). But PDSP could only assist Cal students, though they would try to provide information about community resources to others who contacted them.

PDSP students would soon graduate themselves. Then they wouldn't be able to use PDSP services either. But they would still need help with wheelchair repairs, transportation, personal assistance, and other services.

A group of people started planning a program they called the Center for Independent Living (CIL). CIL had several simple beliefs. People with disabilities were just like everyone else. The only difference was they had disabilities. People with disabilities knew the most about living with a disability. They knew more than doctors or nurses or social workers about daily life with a disability.

This group got a small government grant. This is one way the government gives money for different projects. The money they got let them rent a small apartment, and they moved CIL from a desk at PDSP, where it began, to an office.

At CIL, they started peer support programs. This meant that someone with a disability helped others with disabilities. For example, one person who used a wheelchair might show someone else how to get around the college campus and the city. They could also help someone learn how to open a bank account, find an apartment, or get a new wheelchair.

This thinking became powerful. People with all kinds of disabilities, from all over the United States and the world, visited Berkeley to see CIL. Sometimes international visitors came by the busload. They wanted to see how this new idea worked. How people with lots of different disabilities could run their own organizations and provide the services people needed. A big part of what they saw was successful people with disabilities being role models for other people with disabilities and their families. Many people believe CIL was the place where the disability rights movement began.

Ed became the second person to run CIL. He moved the office to an old car dealership near campus. CIL started a machine/van shop. People brought their wheelchairs and other equipment there to be fixed. They also ran a transportation system to help people get around. This was before there were any buses in the area with lifts so people using wheelchairs could ride them.

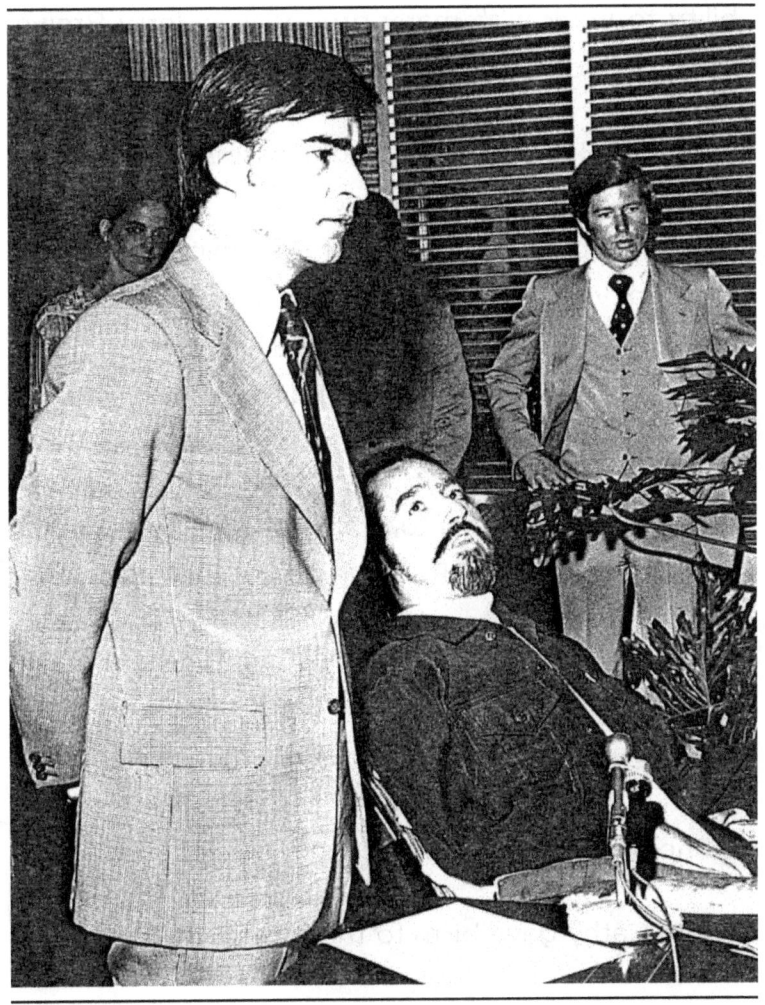

*Governor Jerry Brown and Ed Roberts in 1976.*

As the Director of CIL, Ed built on his background in political science to work with all groups. He believed in collaboration, working with other people and other groups. He thought if groups worked together they would spend less time competing for community resources and have more time and energy to work toward common goals. One person who admired Ed's ability to work with many groups was Jerry Brown, who first became governor of California in 1974.

Several of Brown's law school classmates were also Ed's friends. They suggested Ed be chosen to be Director of the Department of Rehabilitation (DOR), the agency that had once told him he would never work. Brown met with Ed and liked him. He appointed Ed DOR Director in 1975. Now Ed was the boss of the person who had told him he could never work!

Ed moved to Sacramento, which is California's capital city. This is where DOR's main office is located.

About a year later, Ed married Catherine, an Occupational Therapist he'd met a couple of years earlier at a Rehabilitation hospital, when he wanted to learn how to design better work spaces. The wedding was held in the backyard of their Sacramento home.

Ed and Cathy gave birth to their son, Lee Roberts, in

1978. The birth took place at home so Ed could be there to help.

Ed called his mother after Lee's birth and said, "Bet you didn't think I'd be the first one to give you a grandchild." Zona said, "You're absolutely right."

The marriage eventually ended in divorce, with Ed and Cathy sharing custody of Lee. Ed often brought Lee with him on his travels.

# CHAPTER 11
## GENIUS

Ed left his job at DOR when Jerry Brown's first two terms as governor ended in 1983. With two friends and colleagues, Judy Heumann and Joan Leon, and with the support of other friends and colleagues, Ed planned an organization called the World Institute on Disability (WID). They planned to study public policy influencing people with disabilities. This meant looking at how laws, and other rules, could improve the lives of individuals with disabilities.

*Ed Roberts, Joan Leon, and Judy Heumann, worked together at CIL, and later started the World Institute on Disability.*

Ed stayed in Sacramento, trying to sell his house there, when WID began in Berkeley in 1983. This was a hard time for him. It was not easy to find PAs in Sacramento. Now that he no longer worked in state government, he wanted to be back in Berkeley. He finally decided to go back to Berkeley and join WID before the sale of his house.

Zona asked Ed if he wanted to move in with her. She was alone and Ed was between jobs. He moved in with his mother once more.

After Ed was back in Berkeley he got a call from the MacArthur Foundation. A Foundation is an organization that uses its money to support projects and people it believes in. The MacArthur Foundation asked Ed to accept their "genius" Fellowship. This is a five year award. It helps people, like Ed, who have ideas that are new to society, to pursue their dreams without worrying about money.

Part of the money goes to a program of the "genius's" choice. Ed used it to help WID build its programs looking at public policies.

After a few years, Zona began to dislike her lack of space at home. Ed and his PAs had taken over the downstairs. Zona couldn't have friends over like she had before Ed moved in. They thought about making their house bigger, but it cost too much. They agreed to look for another place together and found a house in Berkeley.

It had a separate apartment in the back where Ed could live, so both of them would have their own living spaces. They moved there in 1991. Zona had started consulting, calling herself a Family Disability Counselor, and she continued doing that as well as traveling to visit friends and family.

Ed stayed President of WID for the rest of his life. He also became a world traveler. Many people wanted to hear him speak about his lifetime of achievements.

He talked with politicians and people with disabilities. He also spoke with people who had little experience with disability.

Toward the end of his life, when people from all over the world asked Ed what he liked to be called, he usually replied "Dad."

He often talked about how every single person had something to offer other people. It did not matter how disabled someone might look.

Ed became famous to many people as the Father of the modern Disability Rights Movement. He was often interviewed for TV programs, radio shows and videos.

One March morning in 1995, Ed had just finished breakfast. Jonathan, his PA, held up a pair of pants and asked Ed if those were the ones he wanted for the day. Ed dropped his mouthstick in an unusual way. By the time Jonathan reached him, Ed was dead. No one knew why Ed died, but the guess was a heart attack.

Zona was visiting another son, Ron, and his family in Hawai`i. She came back to Berkeley right away. She opened up their house to family and friends. Their home was filled with people, food, and memories.

Within a few days, a memorial service was held. So many people came that one of the few places in Berkeley big enough to fit everyone was a gym on the Cal campus.

# CHAPTER 12
## LEGACIES

After Ed passed away, people from all over the world wrote and talked about how important he was to them. Ed Roberts left many legacies-actions that continued to have an impact after his death. His life has had a lasting effect.

When Ed went to college he led the way for thousands, if not millions, of others to change their lives.

The Physically Disabled Students Program (now called the Disabled Students' Program), was the first of its kind. Now almost every university and community college has a program like it, serving students with all disabilities.

The Center for Independent Living was the first organization of its kind. There are now hundreds of independent living centers in the United States and across the world.

Ed became the first person with his kind of disability to lead a state Vocational Rehabilitation agency. Many more have followed in his path.

The World Institute on Disability has grown from

three people in 1983, to being known throughout the world for many groundbreaking activities.

Ed also led the way for others to get awards. Other people with disabilities have gotten the MacArthur Genius Fellowship since Ed in 1984.

Shortly after Ed's death, community leaders and representatives of disability organizations met to discuss how to honor Ed's memory. They decided to build a campus, including many of the organizations Ed worked with, to honor Ed's belief in collaboration and to ensure continued support for these organizations. In 2008, seven disability organizations, all with roots in the independent living movement, successfully fulfilled their goal with a groundbreaking ceremony to begin the building of the Ed Roberts Campus. Next to a BART (Bay Area Rapid Transit) subway terminal, the Ed Roberts Campus had its grand opening in 2011.

But Ed's legacy may live on most in the individuals he met.

At a memorial service held at WID shortly after Ed's death, a woman told the story of how her parents had moved to the United States from another country after she became disabled. She was in a hospital in the San Francisco area. She didn't know what to do with herself.

When her family asked if she wanted anything, she said she'd like to meet Ed. He came to see her. While he sat by her bed, she told Ed her story and he began to cry. When she saw the tears he could not wipe from his face, she knew that she could do things that Ed could not. Yet he was a powerful, happy man in his huge, motorized wheelchair, breathing with the aid of a respirator.

She wondered why all she was doing was lying in a hospital bed? She got up and has since become a well-known artist in the Bay Area.

*Ed, wearing a vest he got when he traveled to speak in Russia, being interviewed not long before his death in 1995.*

Her story is one of hundreds, if not more, of the people Ed helped in person. Many more people read about Ed, or heard him speak, or saw him on television. After they did, they got out of their beds, or left their nursing homes, and changed their quiet lives to lives of action and hope.

I hope stories of parents, like Zona Roberts, will become well known.

I hope Ed's story will be told in textbooks.

I hope the fights and deeds of the disability rights movement will take their places in our national storytelling alongside the civil rights, women's rights and other rights movements in our country's history. Most of all, I hope one day individuals with disabilities, and all individuals, will be treated equally and with dignity wherever we may go.

Ed Roberts's empty blue wheelchair is now at the Smithsonian, the national museum in Washington, D.C. Everyone who visits that city has a chance to learn about the history of this powerful and magnificent man.

Ed helped change the lives of people with disabilities and the lives of their families, friends, and communities, all over the world.

He will not be forgotten.

# PHOTO CREDITS

Ed's Wheelchair: At the Hyatt Regency, Bethesda, MD. Photo by Steven E. or Lillian Gonzales Brown

Ed as a toddler. Photographer Unknown.

Ed, by his iron lung: The Advance Star, Burlingame, 1958

Herb Willsmore and Ed Roberts, Disabled Students Program photograph collection, UARC PIC 2800H:007, The Bancroft Library, University of California Archives, Berkeley. Used with permission.

Ed Roberts, Joan Leon, and Judy Heumann, Photographer Unknown.

Governor Jerry Brown and Ed Roberts. Photographer Unknown.

Ed near the end of his life.

# ACKNOWLEDGEMENTS

Thanks especially to Zona Roberts and Ed Roberts, who both graciously gave of their time. Ed did not live to see this book, but he was always willing to talk about his life and experiences.

Thanks to Rhonda Black, Diana Pastora Carson, Denise Sherer Jacobson, Heather Garrison, Joan Leon, and Zona Roberts, who read earlier versions of this book and offered valuable suggestions for making it more readable and accurate.

Thanks to Lillian Gonzales Brown, for support, partnership, love and editorial comments.

Thanks to my daughter, Aimée Gramblin, for being one reason I wanted to write this book, and for reading it to Jaden, who let me know he liked it; to her husband, David Gramblin, for his constant support, including graphic design assistance, and to our grandchildren, Jaden and Cecilia, who I hope will have some understanding of the privilege their grandfather has had to be in the company of such amazing leaders.

# ABOUT THE AUTHOR

Steven E. Brown retired in 2014 as Professor from the Center on Disability Studies at the University of Hawai'i. Dr. Brown has a Ph.D. in history. He interviewed both Ed and Zona Roberts and has written an adult essay about them in his book, *Movie Stars and Sensuous Scars: Essays on the Journey from Disability Shame to Disability Pride*. He also wrote *Surprised to be Standing: A Spiritual Journey*. He has written many articles about the disability rights movement.

He is also a poet, speaker, and wellness practitioner. Together, with his wife Lillian, who both worked with Ed at the World Institute on Disability, he is a Co-Founder of the Institute on Disability Culture.

He may be contacted at disculture@gmail.com

www.ingramcontent.com/pod-product-compliance
Lightning Source LLC
Chambersburg PA
CBHW071647040426
42452CB00009B/1795